The Magician's Tales

Praise for *The Magician's Tales*

In *The Magician's Tales*, Andrea Moorhead tells her readers that "There is no science to imaginary acts." Dream sequences blur the lines seamlessly between mystic places of the heart and the natural world. Her keen, hyper-sensitive observations of the ocean, the rain, and trees "that walk with you into the unknown even if that reality holds anguish" draw the reader into a complex psychological reality. Magical perceptions evoke a climactic essence as felt in the description of a shroud, "Woven from thistle down and snakeskins, dandelion fleece and milkweed. It lets in light, keeps out the rain; it's buoyant and soft as skin." The magical realism of these poems is balanced with acute awareness of the fragility of our existence.

—Silvia Scheibli, author of *In the House of Rain*

Stepping into Andrea Moorhead's *The Magician's Tales*, you need to adjust your stride to match her careful progress from one momentous event to the next. You must not go too fast or you'll lose her and you yourself will become lost in a world which only she can open up for you. Paying close attention to her words helps acknowledge within you what never seemed so obvious before. With her in your steady footsteps, in your more than passing glances, in your dreams without memories, in your hands where you touch either "the slow aching of stone miles under the glistening crust," "the razor-thin marks of eternal fire," or a simple "white rain," there's no destination but where you are now.

—Paul B. Roth

Andrea Moorhead's poems rely on heightened senses and "sudden shifts in attention", endlessly conjuring up "the aching of skin in the black grained textures of past encounters." She not only observes, listens and engages, she reinvents and questions the world around her, allowing language to flutter and sound out, despite being aware of "the stillness surrounding speech." There is word magic here, word music used to capture and evoke, in opposition to a need to "accept what can only continue to slip away." Moorhead writes that "one never knows what will pass by, what will emerge or recede", yet she is consistently able to document and share each surprise encounter, frozen moment, new realization or sudden conviction, her mesmeric poems always "moving into the clear quiet space just below the heart."

—Rupert Loydell, editor of *Stride*

THE MAGICIAN'S TALES

Andrea Moorhead

MadHat Press
Cheshire, Massachusetts

MadHat Press
MadHat Incorporated
PO Box 422, Cheshire, MA 01225

Copyright © 2024 Andrea Moorhead
All rights reserved.

The Library of Congress has assigned
this edition a Control Number of
2024943526

ISBN 978-1-952335-86-0 (paperback)

Words by Andrea Moorhead
Cover image: *Solar Mist,* acrylic painting by Robert Moorhead
Cover design by Marc Vincenz

www.MadHat-Press.com

First Printing
Printed in the United States of America

Table of Contents

Recognition	1
Double Visions	2
Cool Territory	3
Whether the body knows	4
Following the Beach Line	5
Moving slowly	6
The Darkness before Us	7
Earth Waves	8
Effects of Drought	9
Contradictions in Dream	10
Tangled webs,	11
Over the Bay	12
Day Shifts	13
Different Spaces	16
Another Destination	17
Watching the Mind	18
What was seen before	19
Meanderings	20
Other Cosmologies	21
When there are no dreams	22
If White Remains	23
Planting snowflakes is an absurd task	24
Solar Landing	25
Many Lives	28
Escape	29
Other Dangers	30
Along the Appalachians	31
Other Consciousness	32
Zones	33

Saturation	34
Working the Land	35
Beside the Emptiness	36
Disintegration	37
Forms of Fire	38
Inexactitudes	39
The Magician's Tales	40
Above the Pass	50
Gazing Outward	51
Distortions	52
If you are awake	53
Traveling beyond Light	54
Night Scenes	55
Mirrors See Nothing Else	58
Leaving the Susquehanna	59
Mutterings from the Source	60
North of Codorus Creek	67
Acknowledgments	69
About the Author	71

for Marne, who knew the Magician well

Recognition

I've laid out the shroud where everyone can see it. It glistens in the morning sun, shimmers in afternoon light. Woven from thistle down and snakeskins, dandelion fleece and milkweed. It lets in light, keeps out the rain; it's buoyant and soft on the skin. The body leaves its shadow there; everyone can see the dim outlines. The length and width, the precision of muscles, the wild knot of hair. Only the eyes are absent; they're out somewhere, leaving behind lapis and cerulean, azure and sapphire.

Andrea Moorhead

Double Visions

Each perturbation removes a subtle layer, language leaves fluttering, the wind cold; we are wandering again in the catacombs of silence, slipping into passages of stone, heedless of the accumulation of light in the bones of speech, the reverberating assonance of despair or elation; each perturbation removes a thin covering, allows the words to regain force, to perpetrate their understanding of the bond, reversals becoming objects of contemplation, while the ocean continues to storm, and the land sways, trees exploding in the air; we're dreaming now, pulling the covers tighter and tighter, it's spring where we are and the leaves glisten and the ocean murmurs, far off, a noise, a rushing closer, an upheaval of sight, and each perturbation removes a layer, a delicate binding to the bone, that we have learned not to trust.

Cool Territory

Muttering along the fence again, muttering blue and green along the stones again, muttering murmuring, it's too low to distinguish, the clouds are dense today, almost down to us, to here, to the ground, to earth, to who can tell the crows if these clouds are bringing rain again, wet nests, shaky foundations, the night is rain the night is snow the night is all we have and muttering murmuring along the fence along the stones, along the edge of my heart where the rain comes in where the snow seeps where the whispering sighs of crows somewhere so far away so far down the road so far off this Earth this ground this here and we can barely distinguish the sound of the moon rising from the murmuring muttering of your intuition your planted and flagrant degeneration of hope, your symbolism of the ungodly vanished and this is cool territory, it's clean here and elms protect and maples and the shimmering shivering inside your body will cease if you just listen to the murmuring muttering along the fence, along the stones, along the green-blue here, the blue-green now, the sudden and inevitable murmuring muttering, slipping into the day.

Andrea Moorhead

Whether the body knows

if your mind had hidden the light, torn off the tags, placed it under leaves and amber moss, if your mind had moved the light, shifted its direction to the north, covered it with silver mica or the glowing wail of summer storms, if your mind had slipped, moved too quickly, become the storm the light the moss while leaves all around and the green greens the air, covers flight and incomprehensibility, lying in the cool dark, in the stillness around the bone.

Following the Beach Line

A season of folly, wind picking up, dying down, the grass standing on end, flaming, wailing, blades darker and darker, scent of someone walking, moving around above us. Crystalline skies. Your arm aches again, holding all that weight straight out. Milky rains. Waves along the ice line. Twinkling beads strung without care. I hear the noise now. Louder and louder. Ringing on rock, blue-grey on skin.

Andrea Moorhead

Moving Slowly

Details submerged as the tide returns. The thick line of shells gone again. Purple and rose, beige accentuated as sun glistens, the sheen dazzling. We're walking the undulating line of light, flash of electrons in counterpoint. Brain waves are subtle by the sea. We try not to discover how rapidly they flow. Water against flesh. Eyes sparkling as speech dims. The terns continue fishing, clouds slowly into the sun, cutting the light fibrous.

The Darkness before Us

If you pull the evening closer, the dense fibers will show, the coarse hairs of fading color in the veins lining the night, pulling in oxygen and comet dust, star light and the faint glowing before the heart entirely disappears.

Andrea Moorhead

Earth Waves

Eclipse occurs when the sun shatters its shadow, when fruit distilled in autumn air no longer searches for water, and the steady pattering of dream noise enters the morning, displaces other brightness and the mind is closed again, faltering in the sun's broken shadow, in the stillness surrounding speech, in the slow aching of stone miles under the glistening crust.

Effects of Drought

Living in stone presupposes a halo effect, veiling or surrounding the head, as if a saint were wandering off the map, following the thin white roads leading out of rain.

Andrea Moorhead

Contradictions in Dream

Sudden shifts in attention can't mark the surge of the tide, the coastal road is low, inundation from recent rain prefigures this arrangement, this saturation of imagined time, whenever the white rain obscures the heart and you're rolling along the low road, tires whirring in the salt water sloshing from side to side, and the pull isn't all that great, despite great warnings at night when dreams are dislocated from sleep and the night sky has floating images detached from any known context.

Tangled webs,

the threads are no longer clear, red glowing in the dusk or iridescent green at night, you can't see all the threads tangling, the wind catches the edges of the fibers, lifts off the eyes, sweeps away the lungs, muscles, aching hearts, and all we see is the wild whiteness between the veins, impenetrable and beyond discussion, evening rains fill the reservoirs, reduce the snow trails in the deep pine woods, there are blue shadows on the stream tonight, bending the edges of stone and fern, believing that the summer sun has locked itself in a trance, sleeping on the cool neon breeze of the melting snow.

Andrea Moorhead

Over the Bay

Up on the rocky neck, the spine, the solid protrusion, the trees grow tall, silver skinned and luminous, over the river, over the bay, over the next sequence of dreams you had imagined, once on the shore, in the blue-green waters, in the cold mist behind the terns, wavering as you moved off shore, flickering and shimmering, up on the rocky neck, the spine, the solid protrusion, the beech keep their leaves, walk around with the young oak, red-leaved and solid, some night you'll see them moving about, it's very curious, very strange, and people don't like to admit that beech and oak, young and old, go off walking in the deep velour of night, coming home again when the grey dawn, when the rising fog, when the swiftness of the black duck passes above their hearts.

Day Shifts

#1

Certain things tend to shift in the day. Images wandering the night lose their crystalline structure, the blank angles that push the mind into hyperspace. There is less certainty during the day hours, sun glares on the windowpanes, tree branches tilt shadows too far to the north, and I can't see whether or not the weather vane has swung around again. It could rain tomorrow or even as soon as tonight, but I'll not look out the window at night, it's too disturbing. One never knows what will pass by, what will emerge or recede.

#2

Night watch now, all flushed and cold air seeping through the glass. I've turned over again, wrapped the blanket up around me, leaving only the very top of my head, eyes still woolen and translucent in this damp warmth. Sudden light streaming into the room, it penetrates the blanket, causes the red-gold to bounce. I can't see above the wool now, someone has tucked another sheet around me, it's too tight, my head is spinning, spinning out of control, beacons out there and oak leaves, tiny winged creatures up on the roof now, I can hear their slender feet, I can hear the shingles shivering through the wind. It's night again, all cold and wild, my hair stands on end when the windows rattle, when the door quivers against the night.

#3

Is it day now or still night turning into day, who could tell me the difference? They all seem to know, to discern, to estimate the web of hours and calculate the flow of light and stars, the gritty sweep of the morning air when rain arrives too soon. But I'm asking something more stable than all of that, something profound, at least to me, to my shadowy existence, to my phantom lives that are accumulating in the back shed. Is it day now or is it still night? The light around my head seems to indicate that night has been co-opted, that dawn did indeed emerge from that wild dreamscape, from the tangled assaults of alien creatures that dare enter my bedroom, that dared infiltrate my mind, my conscious comprehension of what is and what is not in this room, so who could tell me the difference, is it day again or night again, what has become of the sun-rain or the bitter blue blast of a winter moon?

Andrea Moorhead

Different Spaces

Snow fields. Shadows. Words without weight sinking softly beneath the surface. You can't break the crust like that. The ice will cut your ankles. Scraping skin, scattering crystals. The magic wand never moves now. Space around, space within. Something still rattles when you speak. A fast streaming of sound. This isn't anything sophisticated. It could be someone speaking so simply that no one hears, no one listens, no one wants to respond. Invisible scenes overlay, sound patterns cross the shadows.

Another Destination

What's this muttering, vanishing, aching sigh beside your illness, your withdrawal from sun and stars, this captured flush of rain in the sky, this impossible darkness you have nurtured all through the night, turning, twisting, forming syllables no one can hear, your ears are all wild tonight, out on the light streaks, out on the moon-rock-darkness, the bitter pungency of vegetation getting in your way, filling your throat this passage comes at a strange time, what's this muttering all through your illness, your aversion to sun and wind, the cataclysmic reinterpretation of anonymity, one day at a time, you aren't searching for the roof anymore, the slate-edged roof that defines your habitation, and, yes, this sound under the rain belongs to you, follows you, swift and lean, fluttering under your wings like the passage of snow, and you can't believe that any longer, snow around the heart and the softest silence remains somewhere east of the last word uttered.

Andrea Moorhead

Watching the Mind

It could start again if we aren't careful, if we don't listen every time the window rattles or the floorboards creak, it's almost a pattern of recognition now, a fluttering of the pulse before something abrupt, and there isn't any conclusion to be drawn, no images adequate to describe or fix this fluid impression, wind vapor or mental haze, it's all the same now, it could start again if we aren't careful, if we don't try to recall the first steps, the solemn progression of rock to sand, uneasy swaying of the water at night; the cabin is perched on the low cliff, it could start again if we don't close the shutters when it storms, pull in the boat, it can't stay in the water when lightning is so close, it can't stay near us although we might want that security, a sense of anchors pulled quickly, ropes taut and then again, it could start again if we aren't careful, if we don't listen and watch, wonder and let out the wild tigers before dawn, before the solemn procession to sanity can begin again, circling the night with its absolutes, its dainty preoccupations, its wanton falseness, bleached and scaled, and we take a last run with the white wolves before we cast off, in the showering incandescence of a million strikes.

What was seen before

A sequence of light repeated in the evening. Following the eyes of night, the quick glistening across the sky. Someone's washing the clouds, moving the air back and forth. A serious purpose. Darkness ringing in our ears. Insistent. Loud. Echoing as the lights flicker.

Andrea Moorhead

Meanderings

Sudden shifts when light folds into skin and solar rays absorb cells, turning the body towards the stars, moving against the tide, the slow beating pulse of inner rocks. Night comes without and clouds enter the blood, obscuring the flow beneath the corpuscles, the smooth sheen of another river, following the dazed spectacle of a shattered star.

Other Cosmologies

Unstitching the roads, pulling out the long rose fibers dangling from trees, moving along quickly, the concrete soft grey today, the stream swiftly by the side of road, clatter of beer cans if the car swerves, heavy dew and fog, ears against the noise wall, the sound barrier, the whistle of a train in the distance, it's yellow-gold, it has petals of smoke and sparkling flowers, but nobody believes there are gardens on the sun that sway and contract, expand and disappear into the emptiness, into the conjectural spaces behind today, unstitching the roads, pulling along the silken fleece of the air, the car hugs the road, trees arching overhead, moving along as we turn around the sun, planting the blackened seeds that survived the fall.

Andrea Moorhead

When there are no dreams

The body knows the crystalline structure of the rain, the burrowed warmth of snow, admitting neither labyrinth nor verticality, windows' sheen as the grid slowly fails, the body knows a rinsing of hot air, a cleansing of particles so fine the eyes waver in their stare, solar baths in the green-gold sea, in the salt-brine of consciousness, the quivering of muscles as the day lengthens, shortens, disappears into the shadow, into the moonlight, the cascade of imaginary starlight, velvet night, dreamless and secure, as the body recalls the crystalline structure of the rain, the burrowed warmth of snow, the aching of skin in the black-grained textures of past encounters.

If White Remains

Hiding snow is never easy, although you might want to try. Locking away the moon in a child's dream has the scent of fresh snow, the adherence to warm glass. Nights remain dense, speechless. A few thousand flakes could rest under your skin or in the hollow spaces of the mind. Nothing too exotic, no mirror image, no reflections. Turning too quickly sheds snow, leaves it blue-gold on the inner surfaces of the eye. It melts there, irrigating the muscles, dilating the pupils. Outlines of stars, crystalline, remote. Entering through the night, without a sound. You might want to turn back the clock, let the snow fall, pull the covers up tight around your neck.

Andrea Moorhead

Planting snowflakes is an absurd task

created by the mind when the electricity is off and there is no news, no proclamation of storm or attack or human failure, and the snow accumulates somewhere, and maybe could be used as a source of water if the grid stays down, if the flashing lights above the moon show no signs of stopping, red and green, amber and bronze-flecked cobalt all afternoon, causing the mind to flicker in sympathy, to forge new links, new channels, so that planting snowflakes in the wind might well be significant, there is no science to imaginary acts, no stalling out of gesture or realignment of thought, it's snowing again someplace beneath the glowing, beneath the startled vapor trails coming from the moon, someone else might have taken the opportunity to get out, to plant snowflakes in the upper atmosphere, nothing else could explain the rose glowing above the moon, the sudden darkness, the imaginary emptiness in the mind.

Solar Landing

A departure from the seasons, from conversation or dialogue, a settlement of stone and silt, the rain still leaking under the leaves, following the fissures from root to stem. I can't hold onto the sun much longer, the sphere weighs too much, bends under the anxious gaze of the newborn calf, seeds neon and argon, the rays perpetually curving around the equator, moving our poles east and west, switching north and south in cascades of water, salt, stone chips from the inner core no one can yet measure. The garden remains under snow and ice, the old fence bent from wind, almost seeming to brace itself to withstand falling branches or tunneling animals. I've put the sun on its side in the enclosure, nestled up against the bricks. The light is mauve by day, iridescent green in the late evening. Anyone walking by would think I had spilled oil, radiating rings of shiny color. Anyone flying over would see the sphere on its side and understand that something grave was occurring.

Back and forth from house to garden, shed to house, shed to garden, down the road to the barn, back up the hill, carrying cornhusks and cattails. I'm thinking of putting them under the sphere to make a nest, as if the sun were animate and needed some soft layer between it and the soil. This time of the year, the husks are like linen, worn from wind and ice; the wooly cattails have split their high shaft, ready to drop their thick fleece. The only problem is fire; the sun is still wild, refusing to admit the loss of its position, the sudden descent into another's orbit. I haven't time to deal with those considerations; it is essential to keep the sun alive, to allow the rays to blast out of the interior spaces, the light to bounce off the sleeping garden, slip through the fence, disturb the pattern of day and night everyone counts on.

Maybe all I'm holding is an image. The sun should be impossible to hold, its great reflection would burn my eyes, its immensity absorb my body, its ferociousness obliterate any space I could find for it. These are not semantic questions. The mind flickers across the temptation of the impossible, the sleek attractive pull of solar gravitation, a refutation of life on Earth, of presence in green and blue, brown, white, and grey. We haven't many choices left. Polar bear cubs will join the antelopes, flee the vastness suddenly arising, the lack of orientation, the loss of stability on the ice shelf, the grassy plain. We haven't yet halted the swerve, immobilized the point of departure, cauterized the voluminous noise from millions of unheeding throats.

There is a thin trail leading from the south meadows to the garden. It has not been effaced despite repeated assaults from time and natural forces. Along the path are the usual markers, nothing anyone would really notice, unless something unusual had occurred, like the river's spring flood, or an ice sheet across the road demanding prudence. When I carried the sun up from the meadows, it bled. It took a long time to get up the hill. My arms kept slipping and shaking from the weight. My skin became increasingly burnt. But the rains washed away the blood, cooled my face, steadied my arms, and we managed to reach the garden without incident. That's why I placed the sun so carefully against the bricks, on its side so the bleeding would stop. There are no bandages for a bleeding sun.

Fables and parables have a way of masking reality. What they hope to illuminate becomes hopelessly enmeshed in tales of other realities, the lives of transformed creatures whose movements provide moral and ethical lessons for anyone clever enough to discern them. There is no lesson in the recounting of the sun's fall and placement in my back garden. The details might well be considered fantastic or unreal; someone would probably say it is absurd to talk about a person lugging the sun up a hill to a garden. Surely there's a message there or are we witnessing an episode of insanity and delusion. The mainstays of reality are fixed. Everyone knows what belongs where and who can do what. But no one counted on change. So I carried the sun up the hill, laid it on its side in the garden, and kept watch until darkness covered us.

I'm in the sun now. We left quite some time ago. My daily life would seem preposterous to some, but no one is listening or watching what happens outside the atmosphere. My molecular structure has been altered but I've retained my voice, my eyes, and my heart. The sun has swung around again. We're 93 million miles from the Earth. I've kept the garden with us and its simple nest of cattails and cornhusks. We're moving too fast now, we've changed inclination, and the rays are emitted in great pulsations now. There is no conversation or dialogue possible. Space is vast and the darkness covers even the light.

Andrea Moorhead

Many Lives

Rain. Darkness. Sound of the wind hitting the windows. Branches nearby. The fire sways now, moves with the wind. Impossible. The door is closed, windows shut. But the chimney is open to the sky and the wind passes quickly. An eerie strain threading its way across the panes, it's not in the chimney. Whistling glass has a peculiar timbre. Who knows, who cares, who wonders. But it's raining now and dark outside. The wind is hitting against the house. Trees slip by, they're out again, missing the howling water on their leaves. They can't remain stationary, as we would like them to. It's hard to recognize that others wander off without leaving their destination, that they pace wildly before this happens, that they sing loudly and even raucously until we come to the windows, notice, wonder, accept what can only continue to slip away.

Escape

It's time to move more quickly. Night, rain, the ever-present sound of something not unlike surf or thunder or rocks sliding. You'll find it easier now. No one around, no one listening, speaking, whispering under their skin. It was a composite material, unknown here. Bright like quartz, soft like dew, a peculiar combination crossing categories. I would have taken some had I known we would be going so soon. It's not easy to return there. Eyes, hands, bones. The scent of something always burning, singed on the edges of sight. Your tongue would swell or be so dry you couldn't speak. What good are words there, anyway. No one is listening, speaking, whispering under their skin. It's time to move more quickly. It's easy to get lost here, there isn't any light and the rain makes everything darker than normal.

Andrea Moorhead

Other Dangers

Shifting your weight could prevent falling off the edge, the rain only added to the danger. Darkness, inexperience, the desire to withdraw. Your body is silver and heavy like some metals. It shines like a metal, your voice metallic and gold-threaded. There are no songs at night along the cliffs. You can't even watch your step, there's nothing to see, no feet no ground and your body shines so brightly that I can't even follow you, so shift your weight and I'll be there sometime, sometime far, sometime soon, sometime along the spindly ridge of my own frailty.

Along the Appalachians

The spine shields the heat, pulls up rain and storms, ocean currents startled from their courses and we are slipping quickly into the dim charcoal air, the powder blue beneath the eyes of the wind; the spine shields summer, refuses to allow the entrance of autumn, spinning and swirling, insistent and flagrant in its protestations, but the equinox approaches and this morning I'm in the rain, raining, in the wind with the cold air sinking, hot gusts pushing across the fields, and words tumble around like ice pellets or quick pebbles driven by the surf.

Andrea Moorhead

Other Consciousness

The ground is weary this morning, frost and fires, ice and water always, and the core remains stiff, divided in intention, unwilling to emerge or recollect the impulse. The ground is saturated with thought this morning, unresponsive to inquiry or assault. Soil particles, root tips, pebbles. There is no lifeline here, no blood coursing through the conduits, no nerves, no muscles. The ground is weary this morning, moving slowly, shifting. There is no realignment yet, no plates underneath, no mountains above, no lava, no snow, no mud, nothing to reveal the context. But the weariness continues. It is a continuum without source, a state of evolution unmarked, unchecked, perhaps forgotten.

Zones

Continued hammering at the edges, destruction of walls, bridges, empty passage, shadows everywhere, the night fires have no smoke, a curious suspension of real time, everything suspended in some neutral or fictitious zone, hammering on the skull of the sky, the slipping here has no relationship with that grey dull aching, that synthetic sizing of the hours, slipping off wind and rain, the wholeness is dense again, wavering on the steel blade, the cut and forged mark of indolent insensitivity without speaking about the alteration of land and water, the retwisted stream beds, fallen rock crushed without hands or legs, but the night air is molten again and sounds linger in the still bleeding air.

Andrea Moorhead

Saturation

Waiting for the weather, for waves of heat-rain and timber falling, for the fragrance of burning air, the blasting updraft of ice, somewhere everywhere, and nowhere still has territory, when the heart closes its petals, valves still numb from the shock of exposed snow, the iron gated compound outside the body, in the still hollow cone of evening light.

Working the Land

Someone has drilled next to the hemlock, someone has drilled along the fence, someone has put in supplies for the winter, buried the sun deep under the roots, stored squash seeds, acorns, sunflower seeds, the bitter roots of sudden flowers, you had better go out and see who is there, stop muttering about red squirrels and go out and see if someone else has been out there drilling along the line of trees, moving the fallen oak leaves into position, disturbing the woodpile, shoving stones out of the half-frozen dirt, you might find a low burning fire among the daisies, an airlock at the base of the viburnum, there was smoke in the mist the other night, and you sat inside reading by the dim light of that old lamp you should have replaced years ago, you had better go out now before it snows, before you lose the scent of earth mold and the vast luminescence of leaves turning to soil.

Andrea Moorhead

Beside the Emptiness

You haven't chopped wood in a long time, the shed is almost empty now, bark and leaves, nesting mice, the thin veneer of activity leaving tracks in the dust, you haven't even taken out the axe, sharpened the blade, the sledge hammer and wedges are rusted now, brown sheen where the heavy iron has split its coating, you are wandering too much, moving too slowly, you're lost again out beyond the trees, trying to follow the deer early in the day, forgetting their tracks melt under the sun, disturb direction, indicate a false pattern, hopeful and illusive, but the woods remain closed, and you haven't even chopped wood in a long time, the rain water leaks under the eaves and you sit by the guttering fire, wondering if birch bark burns as long as oak.

Disintegration

I never saw the rain falter, your face is wet, your clothing soaked, the red rusted light caught between your shoulder blades dominates the visual field, the sudden relapse of attention that provokes undisturbed meditation, it isn't raining now, but you're soaked, your voice is wet, your eyes blurred, your skin trembling, the green-bronze expanse behind the trees is absorbing the light, I'll light a fire by the edge of the woods, if you can still walk by yourself, I'll wait for you, out where rock has crumbled and the ground glows all through the night.

Andrea Moorhead

Forms of Fire

Burning ice against skin, the night wind is cobalt, and the slightest movement shakes the clouds. Teeth glowing under the shadows, they might have been lavender yesterday or sparkling gold. It's difficult to discern the form of fire when night rain pelts the body, when the caravan into the darkness wavers, leaving dreams half-conceived, half-invented. Spring ice burns, melts the outer layers of thought. No one wanders in the hills alone when snow remains and the days spin under ash-grey shadows. Speaking again of obstacles, pitfalls, misinformation, the quick turn of events, misinterpretation and misunderstandings, but snow caulks the cracks, covers over the split skin, the razor-thin marks of eternal fire.

Inexactitudes

A certain inexactitude of experience, a loosening of clouds and showering stones as if twilight had become wrapped into the sun, mutation of atomic particles that no one has ever conceived, a sweeping out to sea of the under-dusting of rain, measured twice before in enormous quantities, overlooking the light fragile mist falling all around us, the sprinkling of blue pollen, where the flowers have disappeared and clay turns deep gold at night, a certain inexactitude of breathing, a sincerity of tone that water never bears, never carries in and out with the sweep of wind, hesitating always somewhere on the rim of the tension, on the curve of the wave, in the blue-green depths behind the ears, sinking too quickly into the amber-brown, into the flat white coiling when the sun is high and skin no longer moves to the pulse of light.

Andrea Moorhead

The Magician's Tales

#1

In the black sleek rain, when you wander too far out, the day dizzy spinning and there aren't any hollows in the rain, water sheeting blue-gold and your ears ring again sweeping the sun-black soot from the sky and the woods burn, burn the night, you aren't going out that far again, are you, the dizzy day still spinning and snow snowing where the rain has cracked off ice and the broken shards glitter on your eyelids, lashes sweeping off the sun-black day, the crusty silence around the heart.

#2

Heavenly dreams, the fields are smoking silver, dew flourishing against the rock, and you haven't seen this before, have you, the tintinnabulation of the bells' crooked casting, the slender wires holding the air, the matted sleep all around causing consternation and bird wings above and bird wings beside and the falls flow into the sky, obliterating the sequence, causing great consternation and bird wings above and bird wings beneath this dizzying pattern of sun and star, moon and projected meteor showers, heavenly dreams in the snuggled vapor of an empty night.

Andrea Moorhead

#3

Surfaces with no mirrors, ground, not water or air reflecting light, thick surfaces, friable if a sharp edge and the sudden reemergence of mineral veins, you haven't taught the children how to fly yet, have you, how to seed the clouds, scatter milkweed fleece, pull along the trailing vines before it rains, thunder and thick black smoke, before it snows and the surface freezes, becomes a mirror again, hydrogen and oxygen; where is the heavy light you trapped, held in your hands, tasted when summer heat became prolonged and you couldn't get to the stream the lake the river and the fish had all risen to the north, pulling along vapor trails of uneasy sleep?

#4

Sunflowers are known to step aside when the rain is heavy the lightning too close, they don't wander about like trees or tiny flowers, gathering the mist early in the day, but they step aside when the air becomes too heavy and your breathing so labored pulls the earth closer; when there isn't any moisture in the air and the ground is dust or cracked clay, sunflowers are known to take a quick step before anyone can measure the distance between now and the assumed place, before the sky's arteries harden any further, blocking the night and the easy fall, leaves into sleep and skin dreaming, breathing, calmly the night long.

#5

These are tales from sleep, from the thick mixture of teas and herbs, certain flowers yield sweetness, others the bitter stem of memory, a tale woven so tightly loosely flimsy dense and impenetrable language and the quick release of sound when rain hits or hail cuts across the orchard, there is no protection from the magician's tales, from the somber recapitulation of invisible movements, tied to the world we see too often, overlook in our somnolence, spinning against the wind when the first words slide into place.

#6

Move over, it's cold outside and the fire here is smooth and warm, shut the door quickly, the winds are high tonight, and the windows heavy frosted; where you can't see, the night is cobalt and orange, ringed with uncertainty, stoke the fire again, it's cold outside and the windows mirror the rising smoke.

#7

Destabilization of language, haven't you been in the high fields, haven't you smelled the pungent, fragile, ambiguous sharp odors that characterize the climb, that signal the clearing ahead, the dense thickets, the thin stand of maple and beech? Toss out the syllables you can't use, this tale has no sound, its roots run far distant, into the sun even, into the vast subtle explosions that no one here can perceive.

#8

Crystalline, cold, etched and you won't touch this water, it's hidden now, a roof for the fish, a landing zone for birds waiting for the thaw, imagining the rise of vapor, the smell of silt, thinking the night blue again, the day pale turquoise when the clouds evaporate and crystalline remains on the tip of your tongue.

#9

Too close to the soil burning as the rain is cut off above the Arctic, bird wings blue and silver against the fallen moon, and you didn't believe it was necessary, running along the strands of Earth, pulling behind you the sudden inevitable, and you didn't pause at all, wondering the rain too swift to fall, too frail to be gathered, too wild to recall.

#10

This unimaginable walking beyond the Earth, the green-blue and white extremities of sensation, recalling nothing before, imagining the swift collision somewhere in the outer galaxies and no sleep can ever fill this exhaustion, unimaginable walking beyond the Earth, the brilliant blue-green, dazzling our hearts, eyes still wondering if the sign of eternal winter is flowing through our veins.

Andrea Moorhead

Above the Pass

This time the wind changed direction, water blue-flowing, tines in the glass where pine had scraped against the frame. It was a tight storm, a blossom-showering cold, as if snow had returned, as if ice or hail, the grey presence of February locked in the genes, hidden in a remote clearing above the river, in among the birch where only birds, where only owls at night and golden-crowned kinglets when sun streaks skin and the bitter taste of wild tea prevents the rise of dreams.

Gazing Outward

A slight murmur at the edge of the wind, in the curl of the evening breeze. Leaves, twigs, branches. Moving along without a light, the shadows multiple behind our backs. Indigo dreams. A smeared palette under incandescent. Fingers slip. Noise of falling, falling water, falling branches, falling people. Tapping the table, tea leaves jostled. The grain runs straight, light sheared off, the rug full.

Andrea Moorhead

Distortions

Tipping your words so far over doesn't prevent them from nonsense or preclude misunderstandings, the basket is flowering by itself, all the stems have rooted elsewhere and you're carrying the night too far, too far out of sight, too far along the broken axis, the split dominion of Arctic waters, and you'll never get back here without speaking louder, without shouting across the void, without screaming all night all day all in-between when any space you come to know will vibrate apart, so tipping your words so far over doesn't prevent madness, doesn't prevent misunderstandings, doesn't seem to go with the calmness you've assumed, mastered, digested until the first blizzard knocks you out again.

If you are awake

It's not the moon that's vibrating, it's your heart your bones your lips your thoughts shivering in the cold wind in the lack of heat in the absence of green, it's not the moon you miss but the burning sand the softness beneath leaves, the day twisting and turning before night finally and the lull in sleep when your eyes flutter and the only sound comes from a falling star.

Andrea Moorhead

Traveling Beyond Light

Let the sun go, you're holding on too tightly, your hair caught on the wind, your eyes immense as we make our way across the stars, you're burning a trail now, the sun fills the sky, fills the void, fills every sound that we could ever make, and your hair is caught on a solar wind, Earth far below, and the blue-green light of immense love dazzles and bewitches, so let the sun go, you're holding on too tightly, we've already passed the last falling star.

Night Scenes

#1

Stiflingly hot here. Inside the tree or the elevator, I'm not sure which. Is it night yet? Sounds have a hard time reaching me. I'm not deaf, though; I can hear the sun, hear the moon shift, hear the stars swirling overhead. But I can't hear whether it's night or day. It's stiflingly hot inside a tree or an elevator. We're going up now, rising so swiftly I might catch a glimpse again, a glimpse again before the falling inevitably pulls me back into the hollow spaces behind the rain, or have I missed something again, no one here, no one outside the light, no one starting up the car, moving the tools in the shed. It's cold at night outside the light, and stars have a phantom blue, a blooming silver that the eyes catch at a thin point, and wondering how to go there, how to climb so quickly and steadily that the light remains and the trees and the elevators no longer have sway.

#2

There's something in my mouth. Orange pulp or undercooked bread. Something caught in the back of the throat, but I'm not strangling. It's unpleasant. Where are the bird flights now? Have they passed New York, have they crossed the Delmarva Peninsula? It's snowing here, I'm almost sure of it, although someone closed the draperies last night to shut out the cold, shut out the light, to pretend that everything inside has no outside. An absurdity of belief. Winter streams down the windows, the panes are foggy, and I can barely perceive the wings of a starship. Over there by the blue spruce where the land starts to dip. The wings are narrow and bright, made from a substance we have not yet found. No doors, no windows. Just shimmering from the skin's surface. There's something in my mouth. It tastes like orange pulp or undercooked bread. Spit on the floor, spit on the blanket, spit it out, it's worrying me and the starship's wings are beginning to glow blue-gold in the rising light. You'd better come over now; I can't tell what might happen.

#3

A broken string of beads. How did that happen? There aren't any beads here. No tiny red-black, iridescent gold, cerulean purple or clattering white spheres. I'm rolling the dice now. The stakes are high tonight. Maybe the moon can move over a bit, things are crowded here, the covers are too tight. I feel like Gulliver all of a sudden, Gulliver without any text to follow. The pegs are silver and pliable, the cords from vegetable fibers or a high temperature plastic we don't know. Take the elevator up, but don't ring the floor. Footsteps, wing beats, rattling along the windows. I can't find the phone. Where did you put it? Under the beads? Under the bed? In the corner of the night? Maybe you'd better come over now. I can't remove the pegs, my fingers are numb. It's hot in here and the wind can't reach me. Did you see the night before? It's not what you think. Glowing along the eyelashes, melting down into the lungs, penetrating the muscle fiber. It's never as dark as purple velour. Did you see the moon last night? I took the elevator to the top floor and the moon was waiting.

Andrea Moorhead

Mirrors See Nothing Else

A sudden occlusion of reality, never spending time on images, the inverted cone of light along the forehead, eyes flash and the sun comes in quickly, rooms darken at night or swallows along the barn roof, isn't the rain over yet, isn't the rainbow the darkest center of thought, isn't the night upside-down, I never paid much attention to reflections, to the cast of features, the sweep of hair, and now grey light snows along the mind, obliterating all traces, green in grass amber, white in blue when snow accumulates behind the day, freezing hours and minutes, while the falls continue unchecked, land mass diminishing, Arctic winds intrude, and I never did contemplate the face you saw, the darkness gathered around the eyes, the swiftness you rejected, the tale of blizzards and ice storms, a sudden occlusion of reality sends the mind reeling, never revealing the trail from tee-shirt time to oranges on the deck is not an act of will, everything glides along the ice right up to the breathing hole, the blackness undulating just beneath the surface.

Leaving the Susquehanna

When the mind goes wandering, searches by itself the dense heat of cornfields, the copper glint on brick houses along the river, when it follows the old road despite the narrow trace remaining, nothing else moves, nothing else calls out of sleep the recollection of fragments, the reordering of sensations. The mind has a fragrance unknown to the body, a slight inclination towards fern and soot, a smell no one recalls without scouring the ground, attempting, trying, exerting force to turn rock dirt leaf mold in a vain effort to see if fern and soot have a scent that lingers. When the mind has reached the high fields, sat on a bluff thick with sharp-stalked corn, when it leans there on the wind, and wraps itself in grass and clover, nothing else comes by, nothing else comprehends, the night is crystalline and pure, the day already gone.

Andrea Moorhead

Mutterings from the Source

#1

In the wide diversity of whiteness, a glancing blow from the faces you know, a careening shift of the wind, green pine needles escaping in clusters, we haven't wandered too far from the center of the volcano, moving ice to one side, grit and silt to the other, all the while descending as the wind noise increases and the faces take on other characteristics, a molten gold band above the head of this cliff eagle, a hawk soaring into the whitening sky, all blue on your hands, have you really taken a piece of the sky, burnt off the nails and hair, left a hole in your wandering as the wind increases and this stoppage of water at the mouth of the river, where the ocean salt has coagulated sun and rain, snow and deep blue-veined fish?

#2

Increasing volumes of air pressing against your sides, weighing on your hat, or bouncing off the sliding arms too close to the ground, as a serpent or a wasp rediscovering the slight hole in the soil, the warmth from a pinprick of light emerging too quickly to seize, sliding under the soil as a wasp or a serpent, easing the warmth as the weight of the wind presses on stone, closes off the outer tunnels to the sun, but the day is crisp and wild and all the wings folding around hemlock or ash, moving into the clear quiet space just below the heart.

#3

No one says an ice fall or a rain fall, it's just raining out some days, above freezing, below freezing before the snow falls or the wind dies down, hunkering in the caves you can't see, somewhere out at the edge of the property, in a fold in the ground, a tuck in the hill, a blemish on a tree that descends far down under the roots, where the wind lingers with flower seeds and sun hulls, a scattering of light in the grains of soil, mica-rose and somewhere on the surface it's still just raining, the snow isn't falling, and we know the wind is waiting in the cave you can't see, somewhere out at the far edge of the property, where the ground dips and the tall grasses sway in the black-gold air.

#4

Increasing the volume won't help at all, the sounds cluster where they will and your ears filter out superfluous notes, letting the wind carry them away, and the dull roar of ice falling in the distance shields the sense, molds and flattens the only melodies possible, the light's crystalline searching, the swiftness of stream water or the silver sheen of rising fish. Increasing the volume won't let out the syllables, they're falling as the rain does, quickly in two directions depending on the wind, no rain is omni-dimensional but it can run horizontally to the ground or vertically along your body; lightning strikes are a different question, the thundering snap of a tree bores into your ears whether or not the volume is increasing or blotted out with the firm sigh of the land, you can't figure out the pattern, can you, it's all too dense, too soon, imperturbably close even when the wind dies down.

#5

Move over and stop muttering. I can't pick out the words. Each drumming syllable slips off, creates a nest somewhere, a beaded surface, shiny like new ice, glinting when the wind blows off the snow and vast eddies rise and fall against the tree line. Inside the house the windows rattle. Move over and stop muttering. I can't pick out the words; the melody seems obscure. Maybe you aren't speaking to me or I can't understand you anymore. I've been following the melody, forgetting that words might be attached to the notes or do my ears shake them off, leave them bouncing in the dust? I don't think so. I think they've moved into a new register again, and I'm not accustomed to such high thin sounds.

#6

Increasing the volume only distorts the sounds, takes out the timbre, the flow, the sudden brilliance in the syllables. You aren't muttering now; I hear nothing at all, or only the wind and the swiftness of the snow in my ears. It's stinging, burning, cauterizing. Shout a little louder, will you? I don't know if you are still there. The ground seems to have slipped again, the stars absent, the sun squalls more persistent. If I call out your name, everyone will be astonished. No one will believe that I call you so loudly, in such a great voice, with no tune, with no words, with no other sound than my voice calling you in the vast winds around the heart.

Andrea Moorhead

#7

If you made no other sound, I would believe you, I would scour out the wind from the cave at the far edge of the property, I would ease the light around the heart, search for a different exit, a more compelling melody, take in the blue air that surrounds you, temper the fires you can't imagine, the flow of a lava so dense that the night burns at the thought of its passage, the sea rising in protest in a vast white plume of salt and oxygen, shedding the particles everyone had thought essential, and I would take you out on the far fields where the early winds are born, where rain and snow emerge from a cluster of young trees, where the light on the moon is seeded, and you will hear the muttering at your feet, the muttering along your spine, the muttering in your lungs without any interpretation, if the fires crest tonight and the deep snows drift, we'll go out walking in the unlight, the vast aroma of another world perfuming our phantom sleep.

North of Codorus Creek

The fragile nature of identity, fleeting comfort while winter snows the brain, surrounds the body with light, becomes an enigma of stone and wood. The flow of a creek. Each impulse in the brain relaxed, drifting in the current. The ice flows along, leaves accumulate. The sound of distant raining. I've put more cherry-wood on the fire, slow burning as the afternoon shifts, light streaking across the fields. It's warm in here, fragile webs on the windows. Is it frost lingering, or spiders still hopeful a passing fly will land, unaware, dreamy and vulnerable?

The woodpile is high. A barrier against the wind if I linger outside, watching the birds, watching the sky, watching the light curls around the trees. Birch branches down from last night's storm. Scattered, glowing. I'll put them by the back door. In the galvanized bucket. They're thin; it was the high branches that tumbled down, shaken and split off.

The extension of self, mirrored in the creek. It's not the reflections on the surface of the water, but rather the intense gloss the sun adds, blinding the soul, preventing any rational thought from forming. I'll walk awhile this evening as the fire gutters down, each step pulling me into the darkness, the overlapping thrust of pine and beech providing fugitive shelter. It's raining again and the wind has picked up. Not a long walk, but cautious along the bank. Tumbling down would be dangerous. Stone and wood. The wildness settling down on the ground. I can't walk as far tonight. As far as this morning. As far as I would like. Nothing moves tonight, no one around anywhere. Eerie. Startling. Opaque tonight. The creek flows and I walk along

Andrea Moorhead

the bank. Cautious in the wind, cautious in the rain. I'll put hickory on the fire when I get back. If I get back. Walking out at night always raises questions of return. Unsettled thoughts. Locomotion. Trance. The quickness of the morning hidden. I'll turn around now; I can barely see the top of the hill.

Acknowledgments

Stride: "Whether the Body Knows"

Forge: "Over the Bay," "Beside the Emptiness"

Osiris: "Cool Territory," "Day Shifts," "When there are no dreams," "Planting snowflakes is an absurd task," "Traveling beyond Light," "Night Scenes," "Mutterings from the Source"

January Review: "Watching the Mind"

Poetry Pacific: "Other Cosmologies"

Loch Haven Review: "Distortions"

Henniker Review: "Mirrors See Nothing Else"

About the Author

ANDREA MOORHEAD was born in Buffalo, New York, in 1947, and lived there until 1962 when the family moved to Connecticut where she spent her adolescence before going to Pennsylvania to study philosophy and French at Chatham University. She moved to upstate New York with her husband Robert, where, in 1972, they founded the international poetry journal *Osiris*, one of the first journals in the United States to publish poems in foreign languages. In 1976, they settled in Deerfield, Massachusetts, where they taught at Deerfield Academy for thirty-eight years. Retirement brought the opportunity to establish A&R Design, a graphic design and editorial consulting practice.

Moorhead writes both in English and in French. Her most recent collections are *Tracing the Distance* (The Bitter Oleander Press) and *À l'ombre de ta voix* (Le Noroît). Her translations of Francophone poetry include the work of Abderrahmane Djelfaoui, Élise Turcotte, Hélène Dorion, and Marie-Christine Masset. Visual poetry is a special love; her photos appear in numerous international literary journals.

Moorhead's poems often develop multiple voices that interact. Sometimes it is the Earth that speaks, sometimes a person. The interplay between different voices creates dynamic tension in the poems and allows the reader to participate on many levels.

Over the years, Moorhead has incorporated ecological concerns and world events in her writing. The impact of global conflicts, natural disasters, and human destructiveness has become an important aspect of her work. The impact of wars and climatic extremes on people's lives is the focus of poems that move the reader towards the transcendent nature of the human spirit.

www.ingramcontent.com/pod-product-compliance
Lightning Source LLC
Chambersburg PA
CBHW031606110426
42742CB00037B/1311